True HORSE St

Miskeen

THE DANCING HORSE

BY JUDY ANDREKSON

Illustrations by David Parkins

Tundra Books

Published in Canada by Tundra Books,
75 Sherbourne Street, Toronto, Ontario M5A 2P9

Published in the United States by Tundra Books of Northern New York,
P.O. Box 1030, Plattsburgh, New York 12901

Library of Congress Control Number: 2006925473

Library and Archives Canada Cataloguing in Publication
Andrekson, Judy
Miskeen : the dancing horse / Judy Andrekson ; illustrated by
David Parkins.

(True horse stories)
ISBN 978-0-88776-771-5

1. Miskeen (Horse)–Juvenile literature. 2. Show jumpers
(Horses)–Biography–Juvenile literature. 3. Circus
animals–Biography–Juvenile literature. 4. Horses–Bahrain–
Biography–Juvenile literature. I. Parkins, David
II. Title. III. Series.

SF295.565.M58A54 2007   j798.2'50929   C2006-902061-2

ONTARIO ARTS COUNCIL
CONSEIL DES ARTS DE L'ONTARIO

We acknowledge the financial support of the Government of Canada through the
Book Publishing Industry Development Program (BPIDP) and that of the
Government of Ontario through the Ontario Media Development Corporation's
Ontario Book Initiative. We further acknowledge the support of the Canada
Council for the Arts and the Ontario Arts Council for our publishing program.

Design: Terri Nimmo

Printed and bound in Canada

1 2 3 4 5 6   12 11 10 09 08 07

In memory of my grandmother, Kathleen Schropher,
and my grandfather, Clyde York,
and to my strong and loving mom, Karen.

Acknowledgments

I would like to express my sincere gratitude to the people who helped me with this daunting project. The distances, language barriers, and lack of record keeping made this a very difficult story to research, but with the help of many wonderful people, Miskeen's story could be told.

A general thanks, first to all, to all the knowledgeable people who write for the Internet. I read countless articles about Bulgaria, Russia, circuses, etc., and could not have put this story together without their help. Maya Dimitrova from Wonderland, Bulgaria – thanks for the information about harvest fairs and St. Dimitri's Day. It was an outstanding help. Guido Leidelmeyer from Rocking Horse Productions – thanks for the insightful view of the Russian circus. You gave me information that I was unable to obtain anywhere else. Thanks to Laura Dossary from the British Embassy in Bahrain, Sami Ghazwan from the American Embassy in Bahrain, and to the Russian Embassy. Ms. Dossary and Mr. Ghazwan were especially helpful, and pointed me in new directions when I seemed to have hit dead ends. Betty Rajab, Secretary for the Bahrain Society for the Prevention of Cruelty to Animals, searched records and offered advice. Thank you. Alison from Letters, Gulf Daily News – your efforts in searching archives and posting letters were most honestly appreciated.

Special thanks go to four women, without whom this story could never have come into existence. Dale Rose, thank you for introducing me to Miskeen through your wonderful article on Equine Heroes (www.equinenet.org) and allowing me to share his story further. Hilary Picton – you were the person who broke through the barriers and finally got this story going when I thought I might have to abandon it. June Al-Saffar – most amazing source of information – this would have been virtually impossible without you. And Vicki Malia – thank you so much for the time you spent telling your story, answering so many questions, and offering even more answers than I asked for. Thank you, most of all for opening your heart to a "Poor Man" such as Miskeen. You changed a life for the better, and that is something to be proud of.

Contents

Prologue

It was the same every time; at every show, between every class. The music would drift to the stables from the grandstand intercom. Then Miskeen would begin to dance . . . a graceful *piaffe*, with neck arched, head swaying from side to side, ears relaxed, and eyes half closed. In those moments, Miskeen was no longer a school horse and show jumper, lucky to be alive after being rescued from a horrible ordeal. He was, once again, a dancing horse, entertaining crowds of adoring children and cheering adults. He was cued by no master, rein, or whip now, and no one applauded his rhythmic, expressive movements. But still he danced, alone with the music and his memories of life as it had been not so long ago.

I

A Changing World

Miskeen's story is not the story of a champion sport horse or a remarkable rise to fame. It is a more important story than that. It is a tale of true courage, patience, unbreakable spirit, and the strength to trust again after trust has been broken. It is a story repeated over and over in the lives of horses whose fates rest in the hands of people, and one from which, hopefully, we will someday learn.

It is believed that Miskeen's story may have begun in the late 1980s on a state collective farm in the mountains of Southern Bulgaria. Dramatic political changes were taking place in Eastern Europe and the Union of Soviet Socialist Republics (USSR) around the time of his birth, and the fall of communism would greatly affect the path of his life.

Farms in Bulgaria were privatized during his first years of life, and state financial support was removed, leaving farmers to struggle with very little money on smaller plots of land. Draft horses became invaluable as farmers were forced to return to traditional farming methods, but light horses were a luxury few could afford any longer. Hundreds of riding horses were sold, often at shockingly low prices, including one bright chestnut colt with bold white markings. In the autumn of his third year, during the festival of Dimitrovden, he was taken to a nearby village and put up for sale.

Dimitrovden, celebrated on October 26th, marked the end of the farming season and the beginning of festive harvest days and the "marriage season." Villagers prepared for the festival and the gathering of people from the neighboring countryside. A market and fairground were set up for the handicrafts, farm goods, and livestock that would be sold and traded for two days. Feasts of boiled mutton, potatoes, and stuffed hens filled the air with delicious scents. Music poured from the *kaval, tambura, gadulka,* and *tapan,* and enticed the people in their bright costumes, young and old, to join in dances of courtship and friendship well into the night. At midnight, the people sang for St. Dimitri of Thessalonica, patron saint of frost and snow, and waited for him to open his beard and release the first snow-flakes of the season.

In times of economic uncertainty and the hardship of change, the stability of tradition was a comfort and a release for the rural people and they celebrated with a passion. For the chestnut colt and the other young horses that moved restlessly in their pens, it was terrifying.

The colt jumped away at first, when people came in to pick up his feet, look at his teeth, and run their hands over him. Large, rough hands inspected him; firm, gentle hands made him feel calmer; soft, ticklish hands made him want to kick – but he didn't. So many hands. He was taken out and asked to trot several times and to stand "square" – posed with all four feet planted firmly on the ground (no resting or relaxing a leg). He endured it all patiently, but for a young animal in strange sur-roundings it was not easy.

One couple returned to inspect the colt three times on the second day. The man had a deep voice, like the water in the creek that ran past the farm where the colt had lived. The woman's voice was higher and full of excitement.

"I really like him, Stepan," she said during their final visit. They did not come into the pen this time, but leaned on the metal bars and watched him from outside. The young horse pricked his ears toward them, already beginning to recognize their voices.

"I don't know. He's not exactly pretty. He has quite a big head and –"

"But look at the angle of his shoulders and that strong neck," the woman interrupted. "He's a good age, ready for work. Imagine him after some training and muscling up. He'll be handsome then. He has a nice, wide chest and very good legs. His trot is free and his action is good. I do think he'd work out well."

"Sveta, I think you're dreaming of dancing again, aren't you?" asked Stepan with an affectionate smile. Their grandmother had worked for a famous Russian circus with the high school horses. She had been a first class artist, performing intricate and beautiful "dances" with the horses that awed both her audiences and her grandchildren.

Stepan and his sister, Svetlana, had inherited their grandmother's love of the horse and had developed an act with *liberty* horses, which they were currently performing

in a small, traveling circus. The end of communism in the USSR meant more open borders and more opportunities for performers who would never have found a place in the old system. What had so recently been impossible was now within their grasp, and neither of them had wanted to miss out on it.

They were nearing the end of their first touring season and were on the lookout for promising horses to add to their string for the following year. The expert skills of their grandmother had slipped away with time and change, but Svetlana remembered and dreamed of recreating the act. It meant a huge investment of time, money, and skill, all of which were hard to come by. But dreams were abundant and Sveta always had her eye out for just the right horse.

"Well, he's not so handsome now, that's for sure," said Stepan, turning his attention back to the horse. "Still, you may be right. His coloring's nice and showy. I like that long, white blaze and the stockings. And his temperament seems good. For a stud-colt, he's accepting all the action and handling very well. He'll need that where he'll go with us."

The pair purchased the colt that afternoon and led him to a van that smelled of other horses and . . . something else. He didn't recognize the other strange smells. He snorted and tried to back out of the van, startled by the unfamiliar ring of metal under his hooves and frightened by the strangeness of the new smells. Stepan held him firmly, speaking quietly in his deep-water voice. The colt slowly came forward into the dark van, trembling, but accepting what was being asked of him.

2

Circus Horse

The red colt soon learned about those strange smells. He traveled for a terrifying half hour, sweating with fear, legs braced against the unfamiliar rocking of the van. At last, the van stopped and the door opened, letting in light and fresh air. The colt followed Stepan cautiously out of the van into a world vastly different than anything he had ever known. Before him lay a tiny city of tents and caravans, trucks, and transport vans, with the largest tent of all directly in the center. It was set up on a green on the outskirts of Plovdiv, Bulgaria's second-largest city.

The unfamiliar scents, much stronger now, filled the colt's flared nostrils. He froze, his sensitive ears flicking back and forth to catch the odd sound: music drifting from a caravan, people calling back and forth to each other, a low grunt from a nearby tent – now a shriek. Sounds unlike anything he had ever heard before. He yanked back on his lead rope, terror filling his heart.

Once again, Stepan soothed him and began to coax him forward. Someone called out to them from across the yard. "Where have you been all day? The show starts in an hour. Ivan's having a fit."

Svetlana glanced at Stepan and smiled. She wasn't worried. They were used to dealing with hotheaded Ivan, the circus manager, and there was plenty of time to get ready. They had performed this act, day after day, for the past six months. They knew exactly how much time they needed.

Svetlana followed Stepan and the new colt to the stable – a long, narrow, open-ended tent. It was dim inside, but the skittish newcomer drew comfort from the other animals standing calmly in their stalls. Some were familiar and some he had never seen before in his life. Five other horses, two ponies, a donkey, a camel, and a llama peered curiously over their stall doors at him.

"Let's get him into a stall, Stepan," said Svetlana. "He'll need time to relax and get used to things before we can do anything with him." At that moment, high school acts were years away, but the colt's training had begun.

The colt would not relax that first night, but he would experience the world of the circus for the very first time. He watched nervously as grooms moved from stall to stall, fitting each of the shining chestnut horses with glittering bridles, bellybands, side reins, and high, plumed headpieces. The ponies were saddled and tied to rings on the sides of their stalls so they couldn't roll.

Svetlana returned in a while, transformed. The jeans and ponytail she'd been wearing earlier had been traded for a showgirl outfit of top hat and tails, dramatic makeup, and a sleek hairdo. The horses moved restlessly at the sound of her voice, anticipating the coming performance.

The show animals were soon led out to warm up in the small yard behind the big top. The colt whinnied anxiously after them, then listened intently for a reply. There was none. Only the sounds of vehicles and children's high-pitched voices came back to him. Loud music played somewhere close by. The grooms were back almost immediately, preparing the donkey, camel, and the llama for their moment in the spotlight. Then, once more, the newcomer was alone.

Forty-five minutes later, the horses returned, breathing heavily. Their plumes and bridles were removed and they quickly settled to their evening hay. Only the colt remained alert and restless. Amplified voices and music drifted to the stable tent, followed by cheers, whistles, and laughter. The camel and llama were led back a while later. Another full hour passed before the ponies and donkey appeared, tired after walking countless circles for little children who wanted rides and pictures taken.

Again, voices and vehicle noises outside – and then quiet, except for the circus people who moved among the tents, talking and humming as they closed down for the night.

The colt began to relax a little. He drank deeply from his water bucket for the first time and snatched at bites of hay, quickly moving back to his stall door to watch as he chewed. For the next hour it seemed that the quiet of the night had finally settled over the strange little tent city. The animals around him chewed rhythmically and a few folded their legs under them and slept. Exhaustion began to pull at him and he suddenly longed to rest too. But it was not to be.

Fed and briefly rested, the circus "family" now sprang back to life. It was time to pack up and move on. The tents were already being struck as the horses were loaded onto the vans. It would be one of the longest nights of the young animal's life, trapped in the crowded van for over fourteen hours, while the circus moved to its next location and the stable tent was put back up. The colt's muscles ached and his nerves were raw. It was the first of hundreds of trips he would take and one of the hardest things he would have to learn to cope with in the years to come. Hours and hours of close confinement – in the vans, in the stalls, in the restrictive side reins. The freedom of his pasture and his youth were gone from that day on.

Shaken and exhausted, the horse moved into his stall again and early that morning, he earned his name, *Miskeen*, meaning "Poor Man" from a groom who tended to him.

All circus horses must learn to accept new sights, sounds, and smells without becoming upset. This goes against their natural instincts to run away or fight back. To teach a horse control, it is gradually exposed to new, potentially frightening things until they are no longer alarming. A horse is handled in such a way that it feels safer and more comfortable with its trainer than anywhere else.

Every day, Miskeen was introduced to something new – new people, new types of animals, new areas of the circus sites, motorized vehicles working around him, flapping materials, hoops and pedestals, big, bright-colored balls, and the many, many other things that a horse might be expected to experience at a circus.

Most of the lessons took place under the big top each day with Svetlana and Stepan. Miskeen was taught basic commands – to stop and face his handler each time he heard his name, to walk, trot, and canter in a circle, and to stop and back up on command. He learned to accept the girth, side reins, and crupper – essential pieces of equipment for a circus horse – and he gradually learned to accept anything his trainers brought into the ring. He even allowed a monkey to ride on his back.

Miskeen soon looked forward to his time in the ring, tossing his head and nickering eagerly when he heard Svetlana or Stepan's voice. He was young and spirited and the long hours in his stall were difficult to bear. What he really wanted to do was run, buck, and play as he had in the pastures on the farm. Now he had to stand and be still and wait for his precious time in the ring. He resorted to pawing when his nervous energy got the better of him, and this was soon an established habit.

Five weeks passed and Miskeen had adjusted to the sights and sounds of the circus. The troupe had stopped and put on shows in Turkey, Syria, Iraq, and Saudi Arabia, never staying in any one place for longer than three days. They were now in Kuwait, setting up the tents for the last time that year. This would be their winter resting site and the entire circus family, tired after seven months of traveling, eighty-three cities, and hundreds of shows, was looking forward to warm winter temperatures and a slower pace over the next five months.

For Miskeen, this final stop of the year meant one more lesson. Less than a week after their arrival, Stepan and Svetlana and most of the other regulars disappeared. They had gone home for a break, to visit family, and recuperate before the next show season. The wild animal trainers had stayed to look after their charges, but the animals in the stable tent were left in the care of a pair of local horsemen. The men were brisk and thorough and the horses were well fed and groomed each day. But for Miskeen, without Stepan and Svetlana there, the confinement was worse than ever. For almost two months, Miskeen left his stall for only a brief period every few days. When his trainers finally returned, he was more stressed than at any other time in his life.

3
Liberty Horse

iskeen's life improved almost immediately upon Stepan and Svetlana's return in February. Svetlana noticed the changes in him immediately. His pawing was worse than normal and he seemed agitated.

"This boy needs to get back to work," she said to Stepan.

"Do you think he'll be ready to start liberty training?" Stepan asked.

"He'd better be," was her quick answer. "That's what

we bought him for, and he's not earning his keep just standing around here."

Miskeen's liberty training was to start the next day, but he was too frisky and excited to settle and concentrate on a lesson. Svetlana asked him to walk in a circle on the training line, but he had to move faster. She realized that he wasn't going to settle and wisely gave up, turning him loose in the ring and urging him to run and play. He squealed and bucked, rolled and reared. He galloped as fast as the ring would allow, and then trotted until he was wet with sweat. It felt so good to move – he didn't want to stop.

The next morning, Miskeen whinnied and started pawing the moment he heard Svetlana's voice. He couldn't wait to get back to the ring. But wait he did, until all the other, more seasoned horses were finished their training for the day. The circus would remain in Kuwait for another two months, but would soon begin performances again – just enough to keep the animals fresh and make a bit of money to support the troupe.

Miskeen had already worked himself into a lather by the time his turn came. He hated being left behind. He pulled at his lead rope as Svetlana walked him into the big top. Once again, he charged around at the end of the training line, eager to stretch his muscles and release the tension of confinement. Svetlana was firmer now.

"It's time to get to work," she said.

But Miskeen didn't want to work. He wanted to play. He ignored Svetlana's voice and her commands, and pulled at the line, charging forward once more.

Suddenly, he felt something he had never felt before – the sting of a whip. He halted, startled, and rushed backward as the whip bit into the flesh of his chest again, then again. Svetlana's hand on the line was strong and her voice calm, but firm, when she said, "Enough, Miskeen. It's time to get to work. Enough."

It wasn't enough. It would never be enough. Still, Miskeen listened, and the real work began.

At first he was trained on his own. Although the liberty horses perform together, they must first learn basic commands and patterns, without the distraction of other animals. Once these are learned to perfection, the horses learn to do the maneuvers together. Liberty horses are riderless, or "free." Their performances involve "dances" of perfectly timed weaving, turning, spinning, and crisscrossing that appear to be very intricate. The moves themselves are actually fairly basic, but a horse must be very focused and respond immediately to its name and each command given by the trainer, in order for the finished act to work well.

Besides his basic commands, Miskeen was taught a pattern that he would repeat every time he entered the ring. He learned to rear and walk on his hind legs and to bow. He was a quick study, and Svetlana was pleased with him. By April, he had learned the liberty pattern well and was consistently attentive and relaxed in the ring.

One day, instead of having to wait until the other horses returned from their training, Miskeen was taken to the ring with them. Stepan's hand on his halter was firm and his voice was deep and calm, but still Miskeen trembled with anticipation. He was a young stallion and the sudden closeness of the other horses excited him. He wanted to move amongst them, sniffing and squealing, striking and showing off his youth and strength.

But this, too, was forbidden and he soon learned that he was not to distract or worry the others. A few well-timed touches of the whip were enough to remind him to pay attention to Svetlana.

Stepan stayed at his head and walked him through the familiar patterns, careful to never let him make a mistake. The presence of the other horses must not ruin all his past training. He must learn that the expectations were the same, even with more animals in the ring.

When he had learned this very well at a walk, Svetlana picked up the pace, and soon Miskeen was trotting and cantering with the others, weaving and turning, rearing and bowing. He had become a circus horse.

The company started touring again in late April, and by June, Miskeen was ready to perform with the liberty horses. He was a different animal than the big-headed, rangy colt he had been just eight months ago. As Svetlana had predicted, growth and work had developed him into a handsome animal, muscular and gleaming with good health. His chestnut coat and startling white blaze and stockings were immaculately groomed. His mane and tail were full and heavy. He was not as refined as the other horses in the show, most of them being Arabians, but what he lacked in beauty, he made up for in sheer *presence* – that special quality that makes an animal stand out over all others. He was a proud, young stallion and everyone took notice of him when he entered the ring.

The cheering crowd momentarily distracted Miskeen that first night. This was a small, single-ring circus, and the audience surrounded the performers, the risers set very close to the ring's edge. The great tent pulsed with an energy that Miskeen had yet to experience, and the normally quiet stands seemed to him like one living, ever-shifting, noisy creature. For a moment, he was frightened, but the hours of training soon took over and at the sound of Svetlana's voice and the crack of her whip, he focused on his job and fell into line with his more seasoned stablemates.

Miskeen worked with the liberty horses for the next three years, enduring both the monotony of the performances and the dramatic instability of circus life.

The little Russian troupe performed twice a day, five or six days a week, and in between was the take down, travel, and setup. The liberty act changed very little for the first two years, except for the addition of one more chestnut horse. This part of Miskeen's life was predictable and continued, no matter what.

Less predictable was the weather, which occasionally wreaked its havoc on the little city of tents and caravans. Rain could turn a circus lot into a quagmire of mud. Wind could tear at the tents until they blew down or had to be taken down. Heat could make the vans and tents stifling. Coping with the weather was not always an enjoyable aspect of circus life for the animals or the humans.

Even less predictable than the weather was Ivan, the circus manager. Ivan's demanding nature and bad temper wore on everyone as the touring seasons went on. Grooms and tent crews were hard to keep and changed frequently.

The performers, a motley crew from a variety of nations, were often upset by his tirades. And the animals reacted nervously whenever they heard his loud, angry voice nearby.

It was Ivan who demanded the fire-jumping act that would be the beginning of Miskeen's final, and worst year with the circus. Ivan had grown dissatisfied with the liberty act.

"It is boring," he screamed. "Give the audience something to be excited about! Use fire," he insisted. "The crowds love it."

And so, during the winter rest after his second year with the circus, Miskeen was introduced to the fire bar. He had matured into a powerfully built young stallion, standing slightly taller than most of the other horses. He was showier with his gleaming white markings; the natural choice for the star role in the new act.

Also, Svetlana was fond of him. She had broken him to saddle and had been training him basic riding commands for the past six months. He was handsome, he learned quickly and willingly, and he moved so well. Her dream had not been crushed by Ivan's demands or the hardships of circus life, and Miskeen was the central figure in that dream.

Once again, Miskeen found himself working alone in the ring. Svetlana slowly introduced him to jumps, starting with poles on the ground, and progressing to ever-higher obstacles. They soon incorporated two jumps that he would take near the end of the liberty pattern. The whole process took only a couple of weeks and Miskeen caught onto it without a problem. But the day they lit the burners, everything changed.

Miskeen worked through the liberty pattern perfectly that morning, until he turned toward the jumps and spotted the flames flickering along the length of the bars. Stepan and Svetlana had been expecting that Miskeen would run the pattern, flames and all, out of habit and routine. Instead, he bolted and turned to face the fire from the farthest end of the ring, eyes wide, nostrils flared, and body quivering. Stepan caught him and led him toward the hissing, fire-breathing monster, but Miskeen would have none of it. Determined to finish on a positive note, Stepan and Svetlana worked with Miskeen for well over an hour, until finally, the stallion would stand near the flaming bar. Svetlana praised him lavishly and Stepan turned off the flames. Miskeen was put through the routine once more, and he jumped the unlit bars with ease.

Miskeen's fear of the fire did not lessen as the days passed, despite all the efforts of his trainers to help him get used to it.

Ivan, watching from the side one day, exploded with anger. "Stop coddling that stubborn horse and get him over that thing. He's got it in his head that he can't do it, but if he can jump it without the fire, he'll just have to manage with it. As soon as he's done it once, he'll know he can and this little fiasco will be over."

Stepan and Svetlana resisted, explaining that these things sometimes take time and patience, but Ivan wouldn't listen. He continued to show up during training sessions, shouting at them, demanding more, until their nerves were stretched near the snapping point.

Finally, Stepan gave in. "Maybe he's right. Let's just get Miskeen over the fire a couple of times, show him that it won't hurt, and then it'll probably be fine."

Svetlana didn't say anything, but her face was set with tension.

Stepan and Svetlana both carried whips when they entered the big top the next morning. At the unlit jumps, Svetlana cracked her whip as Miskeen approached, pushing him into his leap, reminding him not to hesitate for a moment. Miskeen jumped faster and higher, confused, but trying his hardest to do as they asked.

The bar was then lit, and Miskeen was put through the routine once more. Svetlana's whip cracked incessantly as he approached the flaming bar, but he veered away at the last second and tried to run from it, as he always did. Stepan pulled him in quickly, brought his whip down hard several times on Miskeen's flanks, and moved him back to the bar.

This time, the trainers stayed closer, striking with their whips at any sign of hesitation. In a muddle of confusion, fear, and pain, Miskeen jumped the bar. Svetlana praised him lavishly and gave him treats, then forced him to jump the bar four more times. Miskeen, now associating fire with the pain of the whips, needed severe goading to get him over the second and third times, but on the fourth attempt, he rushed before the whips could strike, and jumped; a graceless and pitiful display with his ears pinned and tail clamped.

Svetlana was shaking with fury when they led him back to his stall. "That was so stupid," she cried. "We shouldn't have done that. It was all wrong."

Stepan tried unsuccessfully to console her. "Miskeen's a performance animal, Sveta, not a pet. This is something he could do and he simply refused to try. Now he knows that he can, and it shouldn't be a big deal from here on in. There was no other way to convince him, and the sooner we get Miskeen through this, the sooner we'll have Ivan off our backs."

"Damn Ivan," spat Svetlana, and she walked out of the stable tent, leaving Stepan to tend to Miskeen's bruised body and shaken spirit.

Several days later, Miskeen would jump the lit bar without prompting, but he never learned to like it. He still loved his time out of his stall, still ate up the training, and still performed with spirit and energy. But he lost his grace and flare at the end of each training session and show when the bars were lit and he performed his finale, jumping the fire he feared, only to avoid the whips that he feared even more.

The audiences didn't seem to notice this and cheered for the bright chestnut stallion who did his tricks so cleverly and leaped so bravely through the flames. They laughed and applauded their approval when he bowed to them at the end of the show, never knowing the strain he experienced, or understanding the toll it would eventually take.

4

The Piaffe

iskeen began to change in the months that followed. He had become a popular member of the little circus, well known for his affectionate nature and uncanny intelligence. He *was* clever, inventing attention-getting tricks of his own, like opening latches and "hugging." Everyone in the circus family loved him and brought him treats in exchange for a hug – his enormous head draped over their shoulders.

But, as the stress in his life increased, so did his need for a release. He could not fight or run or hide away.

Instead, he paced his stall and pawed constantly, so much, that he wore out shoes at an alarming rate. He was often agitated and grouchy when people came to visit, although he still craved attention.

Svetlana and Stepan decided to have Miskeen gelded shortly before the 1994 touring season began. He was now five years old. Circus horses are often kept as stallions because they tend to be more showy, but Miskeen's restlessness had become enough of a problem that something had to be done. Geldings are usually calmer than stallions and it was hoped that having him gelded would be the solution.

At the same time, his trainers arranged for him to take a short break from the circus to help him recover more quickly from the surgery. He was taken to a nearby stable and, for two weeks, was given a few hours each day in a small sand paddock. He could paw and roll and nibble the grass that grew around the edges. He could stand in the sun and doze and feel the afternoon breezes playing through his mane. It was a small freedom, but Miskeen loved it. This little vacation, more than anything else, helped to revive his spirit for a time, although everyone gave more credit to the gelding procedure.

The touring season started almost immediately after Miskeen's recovery and return to the circus. After the brief freedom of the daily turnouts, the confinement of his stall and the vans was harder to bear than ever. But the rest had helped, and Miskeen endured his situation patiently, resorting to the habit of pawing and pacing when the tension was too great.

Svetlana decided that the time had come to start preparing Miskeen for her "dancing" act. The extra work would do him good. She would start as soon as they had settled into their touring routines. She was excited. It was time to realize her dream, at last. She had the horse and the determination, and the time seemed right. What she didn't have were the skills and expertise necessary to bring a horse along in the art of high school riding. She could teach a horse to do tricks with the best of them, but this was beyond her knowledge.

The high school circus horse is trained to "dance." Known in the show world as *dressage*, the actions are very advanced, requiring both a skilled rider and a mature horse, capable of muscle control and balance. The training is ideally a gradual process of increasingly difficult moves, from basic forward movements to half-passes and flying lead changes, to pirouettes and waltzes, and on to the most advanced moves, such as the *piaffe* (a very controlled and elegant form of trotting, during which, the horse barely moves from a single spot) and the *capriole*. This training usually takes several years, while the horse slowly develops, increasing muscle strength and an ability to sustain the *collection* or hind-end power needed for advanced moves. Only the best horses and riders ever achieve the highest levels.

Svetlana started with one of the more difficult moves, the piaffe. She remembered it as the most beautiful part of her grandmother's act. She had never trained a horse in high school work. She knew what the moves looked like and had an idea, as a trainer, about how she might achieve them. But she didn't know enough to teach it well. Training became difficult and frustrating for Miskeen and for her.

For the next two months, Svetlana worked Miskeen in hand, first letting him trot freely beside her, then gradually shortening his line and the distance he was allowed to move. She used her dressage whip to urge him to keep trotting, as she shortened the side reins, forcing his neck into an unnaturally tight arch. This, and a firm hold on his head, prevented him from rushing forward. Miskeen tried his best, but did not understand what Svetlana wanted him to do. He hated the pressure of the side reins on his mouth, the ache in his neck that he could not relieve, the light flicks of the whip on his legs, and the bewilderment in his mind. Miskeen came to resent this work and, for the first time, used evasive behaviors to avoid it, from threatening to kick to rearing, from head-shaking to biting.

Stepan tried to help, suggesting a method he had once seen, where the horse was tied between pillars and urged into a trot from there. The animal could not, of course, move forward, and so it learned to trot on the spot.

Svetlana tried this, using two posts, and Miskeen eventually caught on to the required move and submitted to the work. His was not a proper piaffe, but it looked fine to Svetlana. She gave him treats and praise every time he did what she asked. Miskeen became adept at performing the move automatically, numbly, but somehow with grace. Svetlana drilled him in the move relentlessly, caught up in her dreams of a moment in the spotlight at center ring. She often played music while Miskeen worked, trying to find pieces that matched his cadence. She began to put an act together in her mind, with the beautiful piaffe as its focal point.

Miskeen had become a dependable riding horse by now. He'd learned his basic skills, as well as a number of tricks, and Svetlana planned to start training the piaffe under saddle during the winter rest period. Little did she know then that the training would never take place and the act would remain a dream forever.

5

Bahrain

The circus traveled to Manama, Bahrain (a small island in the Persian Gulf) to set up for the 1994/95 winter break. The trip was a tough one. Although the cool season should have begun, the weather was scorching. Miskeen had been working hard for the past seven months, performing and training daily with only the long van rides from town to town as breaks. He was tired, cranky, and both mentally and physically stressed.

The heat on the island was intense and the air in the van stifling. The trip to the next circus site wasn't long, but it would be hours before the stable tent was up and the animals could be taken out of the vans.

Stepan opened all of the ventilation windows and the back door as wide as possible to help cool the horses, but the air barely moved. The horses sweated and stomped, growing increasingly uncomfortable and restless.

Svetlana came with water for Miskeen. He swished it with his lips and sipped a little, but not as vigorously as he normally would have.

"He's having a hard time," said Svetlana anxiously. Stepan came over and rubbed Miskeen's damp neck. Miskeen turned his head and nipped irritably at the hand.

"He's certainly grumpy. He'll feel better once we get him off this van. It shouldn't be much longer. Did he drink?"

"Not much."

"Keep offering it – he'll need it. He has to be ready for the afternoon matinee and the evening show by tomorrow."

Nearly two more hours passed before the stable tent was up and the horses were unloaded. The air inside the tent was still and warm, hardly a relief at all. Miskeen moved restlessly around his stall, feeling cramped and anxious. When a groom approached him with a handful of alfalfa and some water, Miskeen moved to the back of his stall and pinned his ears flat. This was most unusual for Miskeen, who was well known for his friendliness.

Svetlana and Stepan sponged Miskeen down with cool water to help relieve his heat stress. As they moved on to other horses, Miskeen nibbled halfheartedly at his feed and drank a little, but he didn't have his normal appetite, even so late in the morning. The sponging had helped a little though, and he folded his legs under him to sleep for a while.

Curious townsfolk were soon poking their heads into the tents to see the animals. Most of the circus workers were busy setting up the big top and tending to the animals that lived permanently in the beast wagons. The few people still in the stable tent kept an eye on the visitors, but did not interfere so long as they were being respectful.

"Poor creatures," said one woman in a thick British accent. "It's so hot. There should be a law against making animals perform like this."

Her companion answered, "There should be a law against making animals perform at all. I've heard that the training methods some of these circuses use are brutal. No self-respecting animal lover would pay to attend this nonsense."

Stepan was nearby, caring for a hot horse as the conversation continued. He had been arguing in defense of the circus for many years now as growing concern for the welfare of the animals swayed public opinion. He was tired, but still, he couldn't just let this go. He approached the women with a smile.

"I couldn't help hearing you talk about our animals," he said.

The women flushed, but looked back at him defensively.

"I assure you, our animals receive the best care we can offer and our training methods are very humane. We invest far too much in them to brutalize them. I've heard nasty stories too, but speaking on behalf of ourselves and most other circuses, things are not as terrible as you think."

"That's hard to believe, judging by the state of these horses. They look exhausted."

"They are," Stepan answered honestly. "They've just had a long trip. They need to rest and cool off, but they are in excellent condition and well accustomed to travel. By tomorrow they'll be eager to get into the ring."

One of the women rolled her eyes and let out a long, huffy breath. "What choice will they have?" she said.

"And what about the 'wild' animals? You can't convince me they like doing the humiliating things you ask of them. I'm sorry if you don't agree, but you need to face the facts. The way you treat them is *inhumane!*" She turned on her heel, pulling her companion with her.

As they walked off, Stepan heard them mention the SPCA. He sighed. This was becoming a routine wherever they went. Demonstrations, accusations, sometimes even violence. He didn't blame people for their concern, but he wished they would understand that most of the circus people were animal lovers, too. But public opinion was increasingly against them – especially where the wild animal acts were concerned. It was getting harder and harder to make a living in a small circus like theirs.

6

The Accident

True to Stepan's word, most of the horses had recovered from the stressful journey and were ready to perform when the big top opened the next afternoon. Miskeen was not yet quite himself, but Svetlana decided that getting him out of his stall and moving would help cheer him up, so she prepared him, along with the others, for the liberty performance.

Miskeen was glad to be out of his stall, but he had difficulty focusing on his performance. He shook his head from side to side, fighting the pressure of the bit and the side reins. He swished his tail irritably when Svetlana cued him to turn and follow a line of horses. This was very unlike Miskeen, who was usually so willing to do whatever was asked of him. He had broken into a hard sweat by the end of the performance, which was also unusual. Svetlana was concerned.

The circus vet checked Miskeen over, but nothing was found to be obviously wrong.

"He may just be having a hard time with the climate. Why don't you rest him tonight, keep him cooled down, and see how he seems tomorrow."

Svetlana and Stepan worked tirelessly, sponging Miskeen and the other horses, topping up water buckets, and working with the grooms to keep their charges as clean and comfortable as possible.

Miskeen dozed as his stablemates left to perform that evening; another sign of trouble. He normally hated to be left behind, whinnying and biting at his stall walls impatiently. This night, he picked at his feed and slept, uncaring, as distant sounds of the cheering crowd drifted through the stable.

Svetlana checked on Miskeen several times that night. He remained quiet, but not in any apparent distress.

When the grooms entered in the morning, Miskeen was waiting for his breakfast feed, pawing in his usual, impatient way. He dove into it with his normal enthusiasm, but did not entirely clean it up. There was certain improvement, if not yet a full recovery. He nickered when Svetlana came into his stall and she was thrilled to see him nip playfully at Stepan as he ran his hands over Miskeen's body, checking once more for signs of trouble.

"It got a bit cooler last night. Maybe it was enough to bring him around. In any case, he's definitely getting back on track," said Stepan, giving the horse an affectionate pat.

"Thank goodness. I was getting really worried," said Svetlana. "Do you think we should keep him back one more night?"

"I don't know. Let's leave him be and see how he makes out through the day. We can decide later. It's starting to warm up again already." They left Miskeen and the other horses to their breakfasts.

The stable tent was quiet when the boy slipped in later that morning. Most of the circus people were resting or helping to prepare for the afternoon show. The horses were dozing or nibbling their feed. The temperature had risen considerably, and, in his stall, Miskeen pawed and stomped his feet at an unseen enemy.

Miskeen heard the noise before he saw anything. His stablemates were suddenly restless, moving anxiously in their stalls. Sharp commands yelled in a young voice split the air, followed by peals of childish laughter. Curious, Miskeen moved to the front of his enclosure and peered over the door. A young boy of nine or ten years, was going from stall to stall, trying to make the horses do tricks. When the animals didn't obey him, the boy threw small sticks and stones at them, making them jump and move about.

Soon the boy found a longer stick and began to tease the animals with it, striking them on the flanks and forcing them to circle their stalls in fear. He spotted Miskeen and moved quickly to his stall.

"I saw you yesterday," shouted the boy. "You can dance. Dance for me! Dance, horse." He poked Miskeen with the stick and hit him with it whenever Miskeen moved near enough. Miskeen scooted to the back of the stall and would not move. The boy went away, but was soon back with a long whip he had found.

"Come on, horse. Do what I say. Dance. Dance!" The whip stung Miskeen as it flicked ever harder against his legs, hindquarters, and sides. Miskeen wheeled away and circled his stall at a dangerous speed, only to feel the whip strike harder. He pinned his ears and kicked, squealing with pain and fear.

The boy laughed and teased more fervently. Miskeen struck out with his legs as the whip burned his chest and forelegs with its lash.

"Yes, rear up, horse. I've seen you do it. Do it for me, now!"

Miskeen spun and dashed around his stall to try to get away from the unrelenting bite of the whip. He snapped at it, ran from it, kicked and struck at it, but the fiery pain would not go away. The boy laughed and leaned further into the stall.

Suddenly, there were voices from the other end of the tent and the boy hesitated and turned to see two men moving quickly toward him. In that same instant, Miskeen charged at his tormentor in fury, grabbed him by the shoulder with his teeth, pulled him over the stall door, and flung him against a wall. The boy lay deathly still.

7

Retribution

Stepan and the groom with him ran to Miskeen's stall and flung open the door. Miskeen cowered, wild-eyed and sweating, in a corner. The boy lay crumpled against a wall, his whip close by.

Within half an hour, the stable tent was buzzing with people and activity. An ambulance had arrived and the paramedics were preparing to move the injured child. His father hovered nearby, visibly shaken. The police stood to one side with Stepan and the groom, gathering information about the accident. The circus family, shocked and disbelieving, came to view the

45

scene, support each other, and cry. Even Ivan was subdued for once. Svetlana stayed with the horses and tried to comprehend what had happened.

Miskeen was moved to a small stall at the far end of the tent, away from the hub of activity. Shaken and nervous, he seemed to understand that something terrible had happened. The atmosphere in the stable tent was as frightening as anything he had ever known. Not even Stepan, who usually had such a quieting effect on Miskeen, could settle him.

Suddenly, from out of the crowd, a man yelled. "Where have you put him? Where is the animal that did this? Where did you move him?" It was the boy's father, distraught with grief. Someone pointed at Miskeen, and the man ran toward him.

For a moment the man stood and glared at Miskeen, his breath shallow and ragged, his eyes wild and streaming tears. Miskeen's nervousness increased under the man's hate-filled eyes and the tension in the air. Miskeen circled his stall and bit at one of the walls in frustration. Finally, the man spoke. "I want this horse dead," he said. "I want this animal to pay for what he's done. I want him dead!" He kicked at the stall door before he was gently led away, but his words hung on the air like acrid smoke. In the background, Svetlana wept.

* * *

In the end it was Ivan who saved Miskeen's life, furiously refusing to kill one of his animals, especially this one – the star of the main equestrian act. But it was also Ivan who agreed on a punishment almost worse than death.

Stepan begged for a pardon, telling the authorities about Miskeen's intelligence and gentle disposition. The vet verified that Miskeen had been seen just the day before and had not been himself, and that he was not normally an aggressive animal. The fact that the boy had been tormenting him was obvious, and an important part of the negotiations:

Miskeen was a highly trained and valuable performance animal. What if they did something to ensure that he could never bite again? They could muzzle him at all times when the public entered the tents and ensure that an attendant was with him. They could use signage, put a barred door on his stall.

No. That wasn't good enough. Miskeen was a dangerous animal. A more permanent solution – something that would satisfy the family of the boy – had to be found. What about having his teeth pulled?

Remove his teeth? Horses need their teeth to eat, to survive. How would he live?

Old horses have been known to survive for years with very few teeth left in their heads. If he's so valuable, a special diet should be no big deal. It won't stop him from performing once he's healed. It's either this, or the horse must be destroyed.

Reluctantly, it was agreed that this would be the retribution. Miskeen would have all of his teeth pulled, except four in the very back to allow him to chew, at least a little.

The procedure was carried out two days later. Miskeen was given a sedative to knock him down, but no anesthetic. He was restrained with ropes and, over the course of the next hour, his teeth were pulled – one by one – from his mouth. He fought as best he could, moaning in pain, but the sedative and ropes worked against him, and he suffered without relief. When it was over, he remained down long after the sedative wore off, shocked and exhausted.

Svetlana stayed away during the procedure. When the vet left and the stable quieted, she went to see Miskeen. She approached his stall slowly, afraid of what she would find. She opened the stall door and her eyes filled with tears at the sight before her.

Miskeen stood in the back corner of his stall, head hanging. Blood still dripped from his lips, which hung loosely over his painful and empty mouth. His entire face, covered with drying blood, was swollen. Blood was splattered everywhere – on his chest and legs, on the walls. A pool of it soaked the bedding in the center of the stall where his head had been only minutes before. A single tooth, missed by the vet when he had gathered them up, lay near the bloody spot.

Worst of all were Miskeen's eyes. When Svetlana first opened the door he had started and looked at her with intense fear. Now, his eyes had gone dull with pain and misery. This was no longer her fine and noble dancing horse. This was a ruined creature that would never see the spotlight or the center of the big top again. Svetlana sobbed as she gently attended to Miskeen and cleaned up the mess around them.

8

An Unexpected Visitor

News spread quickly throughout the small island – first about the seriously injured boy and then about the horrible fate of the horse. Bahrainis are a people of horses and humanity, and many of them, along with the foreigners who made up about a third of the population of Bahrain, were disgusted and shocked by the news. In less than a week, the story of the cruel punishment that had been inflicted on the circus horse had filtered into the many small and large stables that dotted the island. One of them belonged to a young British woman named Vicky Malia.

Although only twenty years old, Vicky was an accomplished horsewoman, running her own stable, training horses, giving riding lessons, and showing a string of her own and her clients' horses. Shaheen Stables was small in comparison to some in the Saar Region at that time, with fifteen stalls and about ten acres of land, but it was well known for the exceptional care given to its animals and the successful turnout of competitors that emerged under Vicky's guidance.

Vicky was as moved by the story of Miskeen as any other horse lover in the area. Reports of the mistreatment of animals always filled her with anger and sorrow, and more than one of the horses in her stable was a "rescue" project. But with a stable nearly full to capacity and a schedule already bursting at the seams, she had little time to concern herself with Miskeen's plight. She had already learned one tough lesson during her short time in the horse business – you can't afford to save them all. So, she got on with her busy life and the horses already in it. Miskeen was soon forgotten.

One afternoon, about five months later, a close Bahraini friend of Vicky's arrived at the stable, accompanied by another man whom Vicky had never met. He wanted to talk to Vicky about a horse. This was unusual, as Bahraini men did not often go to stables that were run by women. They accepted foreign women and lived peacefully with them, but their culture rarely allowed them to be comfortable with having a woman in a position of authority. Vicky was curious to know what this stranger wanted with her.

The man did not speak much English, offering only a brief greeting of peace and some basic small talk. It was Vicky's friend who explained the reason for the unexpected visit. The young man had purchased a horse that he was having problems with. He could not ride very well and the horse was high-strung. The man was rather afraid of him. He was looking for a place to keep the animal and someone who would be willing to work with them both. The local vet had recommended her.

At first, Vicky hesitated, beginning to explain how full and busy her stable already was. A high-strung, problem horse was the last thing she needed right now. The stranger looked at her as she spoke, confused and expectant. Her friend quickly drew her aside.

"Vicky, please. I told him you could help. This is a strange horse and this guy really doesn't know much. He bought him out of . . . I don't know, kindness, pity, something like that. This horse really needs help."

Vicky sighed and asked, "Why me?"

Her friend grinned at her and answered, "Because you're perfect for him. There isn't anyone else. He needs you."

Vicky sighed again. She could never seem to say no to pathetic cases. She turned back to the stranger, mentally scolding herself about needing to get tougher in the future, all the while agreeing to take his horse.

The very next afternoon, Vicky went out to the stable to start chores and found a skinny chestnut gelding tied in her wash rack. She looked about the stable, but no one was around. She had no idea whose horse this was, or why he had been left there. It was very strange.

She went back to the animal and shook her head at the pitiful sight. He was one of the sorriest looking creatures that had ever set foot on her property. Besides being very thin, his coat was dull and caked with dried sweat and dust. His demeanor was one of a depressed and exhausted animal. His eyes followed her warily, fearfully, but he held his head low, as though the effort of raising it was too much for him. There was something odd about his face – about his muzzle.

Vicky approached the horse, but quickly jumped back as he swung his hind end toward her in warning. His ears were pinned flat against his head and the whites

of his eyes flashed. She knew the language well – "I'm scared. Stay away from me or be hurt."

She slowly moved around to the side of the wash rack, well out of reach of the threatening hind hooves, and searched her pocket for the bag of apple pieces she had brought from the house.

The horse's ears came forward eagerly at the sight of the treat and his threatening posture relaxed. He turned as far as his rope would allow and nickered. She approached his head cautiously, placing one hand on his halter and offering a piece of apple with the other.

He grabbed the apple slice from Vicky's hand, but it immediately fell back out of his mouth and onto the floor. She picked it up and tried again, but he seemed unable to take it from her. Her hand and the apple slice were drenched in saliva. Puzzled, Vicky tried once more, and when he dropped the apple again, pawing with frustration, she knew something was seriously wrong.

She slipped her hands around the horse's muzzle and tried to open his mouth to look at his teeth, but his eyes became wild with fear and he jerked his head back violently. Vicky didn't get a chance to see much, but she had seen enough. The horse had no teeth.

Vicky stood back, shocked and confused, and then it dawned on her. This must be the horse from the circus

– the horse that had hurt the boy. This must be the strange visitor's horse. Sudden pity flooded her kind, young heart and she shook her head again, amazed that he would have ended up in her stable. She rubbed his neck and spoke quietly to him as she untied his rope from the wash rack.

"It's okay, fellow, no one's going to hurt you here." Her voice droned on as she led him into one of the few remaining empty stalls. But as she unclipped the rope from his halter and turned to close the gate, the horse suddenly pinned his ears and lunged at her, warning Vicky once more, to keep her distance.

The man who owned the horse did not phone, and he had left no contact information or money. Vicky called her friend and learned that this was indeed Miskeen, the circus horse, and that the man had ridden him bareback from Manama to her stable in Saar – a distance of only about six miles, but a journey that would have included some of the busiest traffic on the island as well as stretches of dry, barren desert.

No wonder the horse looked so rough. No wonder he attacked the bucket of water so greedily when she brought it to his stall. He was probably dehydrated and he was obviously malnourished. Vicky could only imagine what a grueling ride that must have been: a remarkably hot day, weak from lack of nourishment, a nervous, inexperienced rider banging on his sides and jerking the metal bit against his sensitive gums, as hundreds of vehicles roared past them at alarming speeds. Then a strange stable and a wash rack where he could smell food and water, but couldn't get to it. No wonder . . .

9

A New Start

The following weeks and months were a time of rediscovery for Miskeen and a time of learning for everyone involved. Miskeen had not seen the inside of a solid-walled barn, or run free in a pasture with other horses for nearly four years. He had lost his trust and faith in people. He had learned too well about the pain they could inflict.

His final months with the circus had been a downward spiral of pain and misery. The memories of his punishment were fresh and he was fearful and defensive, especially of men. His fear-based behaviors had brought on harsher treatment from the people he had once trusted and worked so hard for, and the time he spent confined and isolated increased, nearly driving him mad. Eating was a slow, painful, frustrating effort that only added to his misery. He had learned to defend himself as best he could.

Vicky knew nothing of his history, but she could see the fear and guess at its causes. Her heart went out to Miskeen and she was determined to do what she could to rehabilitate him. To start, she had to gain his trust; she began with food.

For the first week, Vicky and her groom, an Indian man named Salim, spent a tremendous amount of time simply being with Miskeen, talking to him, patting him, taking him for walks, and feeding him. Figuring out what to feed this horse was the trick – hard, chewy hay and tough grains were obviously not going to work. Vicky made him bran mashes with small pieces of apple and complete feed cubes mixed in, and hand-fed him each meal for the first three days.

Miskeen's first response to someone opening his stall door was always defensive in those early days – ears flattened to his head, hind end turned to the intruder.

But the sight of food always brought him around, and quickly. He would nicker and rush forward, fears forgotten for the moment.

Vicky would settle herself against a wall and feed him, handful by painfully slow handful, talking to him the whole time. By the end of the third day, eager for the food she always brought, he greeted her when she approached his stall. The fear was beginning to leave his eyes.

Vicky had Salim do the same for the following three days, as he would be working with Miskeen and had to gain the horse's trust, too. It took a little longer for Miskeen to relax around Salim, but he came around in time. Vicky and Salim discovered that Miskeen had four remaining back teeth, and that he could slowly manage small amounts of the leafiest alfalfa hay. Much of it fell out of his mouth, unchewed and drenched in saliva, but given lots of time, he ate enough to get by. The effort Miskeen put into eating helped occupy him and fend off the restlessness that was apparent from the moment Vicky had first put him in the stall.

The changes after a couple of weeks were remarkable. The tense, frightened look left Miskeen's face and was replaced by friendly eagerness. His eyes were bright and intelligent and he was beginning to show a real interest in what was happening around him. Instead of sulking at the back of his stall and pinning his ears at anyone who walked by, he now hovered near the door, nickering and pawing, practically demanding attention any time he saw someone. He was still hesitant when someone actually came, moving to the back of his stall, until he was sure their intentions were good. But he did not threaten to kick as often, and he became bolder and more trusting with each passing day.

It was Vicky's mother, Ann, who struck up the greatest friendship with Miskeen in the end. Ann was not a horsewoman in the normal sense. She didn't ride and she had never been at all interested or involved in horses until her daughter had taken up riding a number of years back.

She had strong maternal instincts, though, and seemed to understand instinctively what a horse like Miskeen needed. She had spent a lot of time over the past years in the stable, bringing treats, giving baths, grooming, holding show horses between classes, and absorbing the nuances of their different personalities. She seemed to know the horses better than anyone else, even though she never worked with them in a formal way.

Ann fell for Miskeen immediately, moved by his sad story, his poor physical state and, most of all, his fear. He touched her heart and she, more than anyone, adopted him as her special project. It was Ann who discovered his love of baths, Ann who took him for long daily walks and found him sprigs of greenery in the sandy surroundings. Ann brought him special treats, let him visit other horses over the fence, and patiently nursed his mental wounds.

Ann was the first to have Miskeen's head slide over her shoulder and across her back, crushing her in a "hug." Before long he was reaching over the stall door at her approach, forgetting to be afraid anymore. He was improving rapidly, but he still had a long way to go.

Vicky was reminded sharply of this one evening as she hurried past Miskeen's stall, on her way to the arena. He turned to watch her as she hustled by, then suddenly rushed to the back of his stall, trembling, his eyes full of the old wariness. Vicky stopped, approached the door, and was startled to see him urinate – not with the usual stretching and preparation normal in horses, but more as an uncontrolled release. She did not enter, but stood quietly for a moment, wondering what could cause this strange reaction. Then she understood. In her hand she was holding a long dressage whip. She gave it a gentle wave and Miskeen jumped and rolled his eyes in fear. She lowered the whip and spoke quietly to him before moving away, her mind buzzing with how to approach this new discovery.

The next day, during his morning feed, Vicky entered Miskeen's stall with the whip in her hand once more. She carried it low in a non-threatening manner, but again, his reaction to the sight of it was strong and immediate. He rushed away from Vicky, his eyes and posture betraying his fear, and when she came closer he urinated uncontrollably again.

She moved just inside his stall door and Miskeen turned his hind end to her. He had never actually done more than threaten to kick up until now and Vicky decided to take her chances. She squatted in the doorway, whip held low in front of her, and spoke to him reassuringly until he relaxed a little and turned to face her. He would not approach her, still wary of the whip in her hand, but he listened to the steady flow of her gentle voice and began to calm. Vicky stayed until he relaxed enough to finish his breakfast and then, putting the whip aside, led him out of the stall for a break.

Vicky, Ann, and Salim slowly brought Miskeen around in this way, simply sitting or working near him with a whip in hand, feeding him treats and talking to him until he began to understand that they meant him no harm. It took hours of patience and lots of treats, but in the end, he tolerated having the whip not only near him, but touching him and moving around him as well. He never became totally comfortable with whips, but he improved immensely. It was a big step forward into his new life.

10

The Dancing Horse of Shaheen Stable

Miskeen touched the hearts of those around him with his sad story and his fears, but not as much as he touched them with his more pleasant surprises.

Ann was the first to discover that Miskeen could "dance." She had put him in crossties (a rope on each side of an aisle attached to the horse's halter) to groom him, and walked away for a moment to get her grooming tools. When she turned back to him, she was astonished to find him dancing. There was no other way to describe it. His neck was arched and his head swayed gracefully back and forth as he performed a sort of prancing trot on the spot. He stopped as soon as he heard her voice.

When Ann described the dance to her daughter, Vicky insisted that he must have been *weaving* – a behavior seen in bored, stressed horses. He certainly had other behaviors of that kind, such as his constant pawing. Perhaps this was simply the first time anyone had caught him at it. Ann wasn't convinced.

Vicky witnessed the dance for herself just a few days later, when they first turned Miskeen out into a small paddock. He stood very still for the first few moments, as though trying to decide how to handle this new freedom. He started moving slowly at first, sniffing every inch of the perimeter, every pile of manure, every hoofprint in the sand. He broke into a trot, and then froze, as if he had forgotten how to do it without being cued.

Vicky and Ann were about to leave him to settle in and play for a while, when he started to move in a way they had never seen a horse move before. He trotted a few steps, then changed direction with a quick pirouette, trotted forward again, and pirouetted again. He reared, walked forward a few steps on his hind legs, and then came down into a low, sweeping stretch – a bow. When he rose in the very center of the paddock, he repeated the dance Ann had seen him do in the crossties. Mother and daughter watched, silent and mesmerized, as the skinny, homely gelding performed for some unknown, invisible audience.

Miskeen was often seen dancing after that, always when he was alone, and especially when music was playing. There was no apparent reason for it – he just did it. He would move with his eyes half closed, his ears relaxed, and with the expression of a creature reliving a memory that did not belong to the here and now. It was an intimate, beautiful dance that made his caregivers love him more than ever.

* * *

Time passed and, except for one brief, baffling visit, Vicky still had not heard from Miskeen's owner. She had received no payment from him and knew no more about the horse or the man's plans for him than before.

Eventually, Vicky called her friend again to ask what was going on. Was the man planning to pay to keep Miskeen there? Did he realize how much work this horse was? What had become of him?

Her friend got back to her later, reporting that the owner was having financial difficulties and could not afford to board Miskeen at her stable. He was making arrangements to move the horse to another location. Vicky knew the other stable well – for its reputation for mistreating its horses. She hated the thought of sending Miskeen there.

Ann was thoroughly distressed when she heard the news.

"We can't let this happen. He's made such gains, come such a long way. But he's still so fragile. If he goes there, it'll all be lost."

"I know," answered Vicky glumly. "It would only take one bad experience."

"Let's offer to buy him," suggested Ann impulsively, her green eyes eager and intense.

A grin spread slowly over Vicky's face. "That wouldn't be very smart business," she teased.

"Oh, who cares," laughed Ann. "I'm afraid I've fallen in love with that bucket of drool out there, and I'll be damned if I'll let someone wreck him now."

So, the friend was phoned once more, and an offer relayed through him to Miskeen's owner. It was a very low offer, but it was attractive to a young man with financial problems, especially when Vicky added that she would not charge for the livery fees he already owed her. The man came to the stable for the third and final time, and the deed was done.

Ann, Vicky, and Salim stood by Miskeen's stall that evening, discussing what to do with him now.

"Well, we've certainly bought a good one this time!" laughed Vicky sarcastically, as she gently pushed his muzzle away from her. Miskeen had been nibbling the edge of her shirt, leaving it soaked and green with saliva. "I've honestly never seen a horse drool so much. It's disgusting!"

"I'm so glad he's ours," said Ann affectionately, rubbing the horse's forehead. "Look how different he is."

She was right about that. Miskeen had put on a bit of weight, and his chestnut coat was beginning to take on a healthier shine under Ann's daily grooming. His thick mane and tail, conditioned and combed, hung smooth and heavy. He seemed to be changing with each passing day, showing more and more the sweet, friendly, intelligent personality that had once made him a favorite with the Russian circus crew.

"There is one more change we need to make, though," Ann said. "Miskeen is no name for a nice horse like this. He's had enough of being a Poor Man." She leaned forward and kissed the velvety muzzle. "You are now, officially our own Brandy Snap. Welcome to the family."

"What will you do with him?" asked Salim, when he had stopped laughing. "Do you think he can be ridden?"

Vicky eyed the horse thoughtfully, then answered, "Well, if that man was able to ride him bareback through all that Manama traffic, I'd say he's probably trained well enough. We'll need to find out how much he knows. I'll start playing around with him, now that he's ours. In the meantime, I think he could use a little paddock time with some pals of his own."

"What, out in the big field?" said Salim doubtfully. "Do you think he can manage that? He won't be able to defend himself very well."

"Oh, I have a feeling he'll take care of himself just fine," answered Vicky, remembering her first experiences with him. "But we'll introduce him slowly, just in case. I'll start him out with Sundance and we'll go from there."

Sundance was Vicky's first and favorite horse – a stocky, big-bellied, chestnut cob bought for her by her father when she was sixteen. He was the beginning of all things "horse" for her, including the stable she now ran, and she trusted him implicitly.

The next morning, Sundance was waiting in the paddock when Brandy Snap was led out. Sundance was a bold and friendly little fellow and he wasted no time rushing up to Brandy Snap, eager to investigate this new stablemate. Brandy Snap was used to having other horses around, but not in such unconfined space. He scooted around Sundance nervously as Sundance tried to sniff him and "talk" to him. It had been years since he had socialized freely with another horse. Overwhelmed, Brandy Snap turned his rump to Sundance and warned him to back off. Sundance heeded the warning, and unoffended, turned his attention to the bits of alfalfa Vicky had scattered in the arena for them.

Slowly, Brandy Snap approached Sundance, and Sundance, now busy sifting leaves from the sand, patiently allowed the strange newcomer to check him all over. It took time for old memories and instincts to override what had been learned during the circus years. Brandy Snap tentatively moved alongside the smaller gelding and nuzzled his neck. Instantly, Sundance returned the gesture and, within minutes, they were employed happily in mutual grooming, something Brandy Snap had not experienced since his days as a colt. It didn't seem to matter to Sundance that Brandy Snap wasn't doing a very good job of his part of the grooming. Without teeth, Brandy Snap couldn't scratch very well, and ended up soaking Sundance's neck and withers. But he did his best, and they both seemed to enjoy it.

Grooming turned into playful nibbling, and soon the pair was engaged in chasing each other, rearing, kicking, and biting – all in fun. The play-fight lasted for more than twenty minutes before the pair finally tired and stood, muzzle to muzzle, resting together. For the

first time in four years, Brandy Snap had a friend of his own kind.

One by one, the other geldings of the stable were introduced, and before long, Brandy Snap was a member of the gelding herd. The large paddock was the perfect place for him as there was no grass for any of them to graze – only sand. He could paw to his heart's content, and roll and run and play. He could lie in the sun with the other geldings and fully relax in a way that he had not done in years. He had been given more than just a little freedom. He had been given back his life.

The other geldings soon learned that they could pester Brandy Snap without fear of being hurt. He would bite them with everything he had, but the worst he could do was slobber all over them, sometimes so much, that they needed to be hosed off when they came in. The play-fighting was all good natured, but the others quickly learned that when Brandy Snap turned his rump to them, he'd had enough. He wasn't at the top of the pecking order, but he held his own just fine.

Vicky began working with Brandy Snap in the arena for a short time each day. She put him on a lunge line and quickly found that he understood this sort of work extremely well. He did not resist the saddle when she tried it on him and remained calm while she gently tried several different bits to see which would be most comfortable. He stood rock solid when Vicky mounted, and responded lightly to her aids when she asked him to move out. He apparently knew his basic riding commands well. He did not understand commands for more advanced work, but tried his best to do as Vicky asked. She was pleased. It seemed that his fears did not extend into his working life – at least not as far as she had been able to determine so far.

Within another couple of months, Brandy Snap was a completely different horse than the one who had stood in her wash rack that first day. Working with Vicky and playing in the pasture had toned his muscles a bit, although he was still rather thin. Ann's continued attentions had brought out the full sheen of his chestnut coat and the sweetness of his nature. His eyes no longer held the wary look of the first weeks, and he showed no further signs of aggression, even when startled. He was learning to trust again.

11

Saying Good-bye

Brandy Snap enjoyed the next two years in the sandy fields of Shaheen Stables, being nurtured and pampered by Ann, Vicky, and Salim. Except for the odd shape of his toothless muzzle, he had regained much of the presence of his early years in the circus. Everyone who learned his story and discovered his exceptional personality loved him.

By now, Brandy Snap was being used as a lesson horse and hacking mount for many of Vicky's clients – mostly middle-aged British women along with a few younger students. He had proven to be a well-trained

mount that was not prone to spooking or other dangerous habits, and this, along with an undeniable sense of
humor, made him a steady favorite.

It wasn't long before Brandy Snap began to use his
circus training to advantage with these riders. Time and
again, they would walk back to the stable, horseless but
laughing, describing how they had been dumped in the
most graceful manner. Everyone knew of Brandy Snap's
trick of bowing for treats and they bought in, giving him
sugar cubes and horse cookies whenever he performed.
They soon discovered that he would also do this under
saddle, bowing whenever they stopped for too long, then
looking back for his treat. Of course, they gave it to him.

Clever Brandy Snap soon began to modify this trick
to his advantage. He would bow, take the treat, and while
the person was still leaning forward, he would quickly
step out in the opposite direction, causing his rider to slip
over a shoulder and onto the ground. Brandy Snap would
then trot back to the stable gate, quite pleased with
himself. The riders eventually caught on and avoided his
trick, but for a while, it was the joke of the stable.

Brandy Snap actually turned out to be one of the
safest and most reliable horses Vicky could offer her
students, and he was the clear favorite of the younger or
more nervous riders. He never tried his tricks on them,

seeming to know that this wasn't the time for fooling around. He was easy to ride and gave these students the confidence they needed to go on to stronger, more athletic mounts. The horse that had so recently been judged a dangerous animal was now a gentle school-master for the most timid and inexperienced students Vicky had.

Brandy Snap surprised them one day by "free jumping" a series of jumps that had been left in the gelding pasture after a training session with some other horses. No one made him jump and there was no reason for him to do it, except that he wanted to. No one even knew that he could jump, but here he was, doing it in perfect form.

Vicky had a couple of her braver students try him over jumps – at first low, and then higher, as she watched to see how adept he was at this. Brandy Snap showed no hesitation toward any obstacle and tried his hardest to do what was asked of him.

He was soon a regular competitor at the local shows. He became well known within the island's horse com-munity and he was loved for his courage, resilience, and funny nature. The image of his dancing was engraved on many a memory as he continued to fill quiet moments in his stall with a dreamlike grace.

One of Vicky's students, a boy named Hassan, began riding Brandy Snap during lessons in the fall and winter of 1996. Hassan was an unusually quiet and polite boy of about fourteen years, the son of a doctor, and a fearless young rider. He was a quick learner and a keen competitor, and he was soon as attached to Brandy Snap as anyone could be.

At first, Brandy Snap was nervous of Hassan, who moved quickly and quietly and rode quite strongly. Under Vicky's guidance, Hassan soon learned the best ways to earn Brandy Snap's trust and friendship. As a result, Brandy Snap responded to his efforts wholeheartedly. Hassan thought the world of the lovable gelding and often hovered around Brandy Snap's stall long after the lessons were over, helping with the stable chores, just to be close to the horse for a while longer.

Hassan began to borrow Brandy Snap as a show mount, riding him at first in the junior classes. Vicky readily agreed, happy to see Brandy Snap being used, and knowing he was in good hands with the gentle boy. They did well together, quickly moving into intermediate levels of competition. Brandy Snap was a very able and willing jumper and the perfect match for a boy just starting out in the local show scene.

It should have been no surprise, therefore, when one day, Hassan's father approached Vicky after a show and offered to buy Brandy Snap for his son. But Vicky *was* surprised. The thought of selling Brandy Snap had never entered her mind and the idea caught her off guard. She told the boy's father that she would think about it, but she could barely think at all by the time she went to her mother and told Ann about the offer.

After getting over the initial shock of the idea, they considered it seriously. Vicky tried to be businesslike about it.

"Well, if we had to sell him to anyone, Hassan would be the first person I would choose. He's very devoted to Brandy Snap and he's a great kid. His family is good, well educated, and nice. At least we'd know he was in good hands with them and being well cared for. I just never really thought about letting him go."

Ann sighed and fought back the tightness in her throat. "I know. It's hard to imagine the place without him and his funny ways. But he has sort of . . . grown up, I guess, hasn't he? He doesn't really need us anymore. Maybe it's time to let him move on to something new."

"Spoken like a true mother," said Vicky in a quiet voice. "You're right, though. Something in my heart tells me this is okay. Hassan is the right person for Brandy Snap and he'll be safe and happy with the boy."

Saying good-bye was difficult for everyone. Brandy Snap's hearty nickers, his hugs, his chewing and pawing, his trails of saliva, his funny tricks, and his dancing would be sorely missed by all who knew him. Ann made him a special farewell meal of warm bran with all of his favorite treats mixed in and gave him a final bath to have him looking his best. Vicky simply sat with him a while, savoring her memories and talking to him. She knew she would see him again at the local shows, but she was already missing him just the same.

Vicky did continue to see the pair at the shows over the next few years. They were a successful team, competing in everything from intermediate show-jumping classes to bareback puissance (high jumping). Brandy Snap looked good and was obviously well cared for, and, as he always had, he danced in his stall whenever music drifted to him from the grandstand.

Vicky and her family eventually left Bahrain and returned to England. Tragically, her father passed away after a battle with cancer not long after. Vicky and her mother are there still, although Vicky considers Bahrain her one true home and holds the memories of her life there, and the horses she shared it with, very dearly.

Brandy Snap remained in the Middle East, eventually living out his final years at a riding stable in Kuwait where he gently trained other young riders and lived an ordinary, peaceful life. He did not go on to fame and glory. He won no major championships and he didn't make his owner rich. And yet, he embodies the spirit, strength, and courage of a champion. He lived well into his teens – challenged each and every day by the difficulties of eating – trusting enough to put aside his old fears and retaining the dignity of a beautiful, spirited animal. Through all he endured and suffered at the hands of men, Brandy Snap – Miskeen – continued to dance until the end of his days. Those who knew him and loved him, believe he must be dancing still.

Note to Readers

This story of Miskeen is as accurate a portrayal of the horse's actual life as it was possible to write. His exact origins have been lost, and the information about his early years came to me as speculation and hand-me-down remembrances. The early chapters of his story, until his rescue in Bahrain, have been recreated based on the history of horses in Bulgaria, the typical lives of horses in the many small circuses that traveled throughout Eastern Europe, Russia, and the Middle East in the 1990s, and the few surviving details believed to be true about Miskeen.

A circus did exist and winter in Bahrain, bringing with it the horse, Miskeen. There was an incident with a boy, and the horse's teeth were pulled. But it was extremely difficult to obtain details about this circus, and so the Russian characters, many of the events within the circus, and the details of Miskeen's younger days as a performer have been fictionalized. Any resemblance to actual people is coincidence.

The account of Miskeen's time with Vicky Malia is accurate and true.

About the Author

Judy Andrekson grew up in Nova Scotia with a pen in one hand and a lead rope in the other. At the age of twenty, she moved to Alberta, where she could pursue her great love of horses, and there she worked for six years, managing a thoroughbred racehorse farm. By her thirties, Judy had also begun to write seriously. Now she combines both of her passions in her new series for young readers, True Horse Stories. Judy also works as an educational assistant. She, her husband, and their daughter live in Sherwood Park, Alberta with a constantly changing assortment of animals.

True HORSE Stories by Judy Andrekson:

Little Squire: The Jumping Pony
Miskeen: The Dancing Horse
JB Andrew: Mustang Magic